The Facts on Famous Artifacts

THE MYSTERIOUS MONA LISA

Dwayne Hicks

CREATED BY Humans

Published in 2027 by The Rosen Publishing Group, Inc.
2544 Clinton Street, Buffalo, NY 14224

First Edition

Editor: Greg Roza
Designer: Michael Flynn

Photo Credits: Cover 365 Focus Photography/Shutterstock.com; (series background) Yuliya Chsherbakova/Shutterstock.com; p. 4 Zvonimir Atletic/Shutterstock.com; p. 5 Ewa Studio/Shutterstock.com; p. 6 https://en.wikipedia.org/wiki/Vitruvian_Man#/media/File:Da_Vinci_Vitruve_Luc_Viatour.jpg; p. 7 https://commons.wikimedia.org/wiki/File:Sandro_Botticelli_-_La_nascita_di_Venere_-_Google_Art_Project_-_edited.jpg; p. 9 https://commons.wikimedia.org/wiki/File:Portrait_of_Pope_Leo_X_(Raphael)_-_brightened.jpg; p. 11 (left) https://commons.wikimedia.org/wiki/File:Leonardo_Da_Vinci%27s_Brain_Physiology.jpg; p. 11 (right) https://commons.wikimedia.org/wiki/File:Vis_aerienne_Luc_Viatour.jpg; p. 13 https://commons.wikimedia.org/wiki/File:Leonardo_retrata_a_la_Gioconda,_por_Cesare_Maccari.jpg; p. 15 https://commons.wikimedia.org/wiki/File:MonaLisa_sfumato.jpeg; p. 17 (main) https://commons.wikimedia.org/wiki/File:Gioconda_(copia_del_Museo_del_Prado_restaurada).jpg; p. 17 (inset) https://commons.wikimedia.org/wiki/File:Sketch_of_the_Mona_Lisa_by_Raphael.jpg; p. 19 https://commons.wikimedia.org/wiki/File:Louis_Beroud_-_Mona_Lisa_au_Louvre_1911.jpg; p. 21 (left) https://commons.wikimedia.org/wiki/File:Stealing_Mona_Lisa.jpg; p. 21 (right) https://commons.wikimedia.org/wiki/File:Excelsior,_journal_illustré_quotidien,_La_Joconde_est_Revenue,_1_January_1914.jpg; p. 22 prochasson frederic/Shutterstock.com; p. 23 https://commons.wikimedia.org/wiki/File:Visitors_of_Louvre_looking_at_Mona_Lisa_(40634123803).jpg; p. 24 Andrzej Lisowski Travel/Shutterstock.com; p. 25 (left) https://en.wikipedia.org/wiki/File:Marcel_Duchamp,_1919,_L.H.O.O.Q.jpg; p. 25 (top right) https://commons.wikimedia.org/wiki/File:Celebration_Cosplay_-_Mona_Leia_(17207009788).jpg; p. 25 (bottom right) https://commons.wikimedia.org/wiki/File:Vitoria_-_Graffiti_Gioconda.jpg; p. 27 (left) https://commons.wikimedia.org/wiki/File:Helix,_v.4,_no.3,_Aug._1,_1968_-_DPLA_-_8005c2559d8982847066960b6e94d12c_(page_1).jpg; p. 27 (top right) Aurora8/Shutterstock.com; p. 27 (bottom right) Tim Asadov/Shutterstock.com; p. 28 https://en.wikipedia.org/wiki/File:Mona_Lisa,_by_Leonardo_da_Vinci,_from_C2RMF_retouched.jpg; p. 29 Gorodenkoff/Shutterstock.com.

Cataloging-in-Publication Data

Names: Hicks, Dwayne.
Title: The mysterious Mona Lisa / Dwayne Hicks.
Description: Buffalo, New York : Created by Humans, an imprint of Rosen Publishing, 2027. | Series: The facts on famous artifacts | Includes glossary and index.
Identifiers: ISBN 9781534553224 (pbk.) | ISBN 9781534553231 (library bound) | ISBN 9781534553248 (ebook)
Subjects: LCSH: Leonardo, da Vinci, 1452-1519. Mona Lisa--Juvenile literature. | Painting, Modern--Juvenile literature.
Classification: LCC ND623.L5 H53 2027 | DDC 759.06--dc23

Manufactured in the United States of America

CPSIA Compliance Information: Batch #CSCBH27. For Further Information contact Rosen Publishing at 1-800-237-9932.

CONTENTS

A FAMILIAR FACE

The *Mona Lisa* is probably the world's most talked-about painting. The portrait of the woman with the mysterious smile has appeared on countless products over the years: posters, T-shirts, coffee mugs, candies, and much more. The painting has been copied, **parodied**, and used to advertise many products.

Created in Italy by Renaissance painter Leonardo da Vinci, the *Mona Lisa* now lives permanently in the Louvre Museum in Paris, France. It is estimated to be worth $800 million! The **mystique** surrounding this famous painting has grown over the years due to the sense of mystery and awe it instills in viewers.

LEONARDO DA VINCI

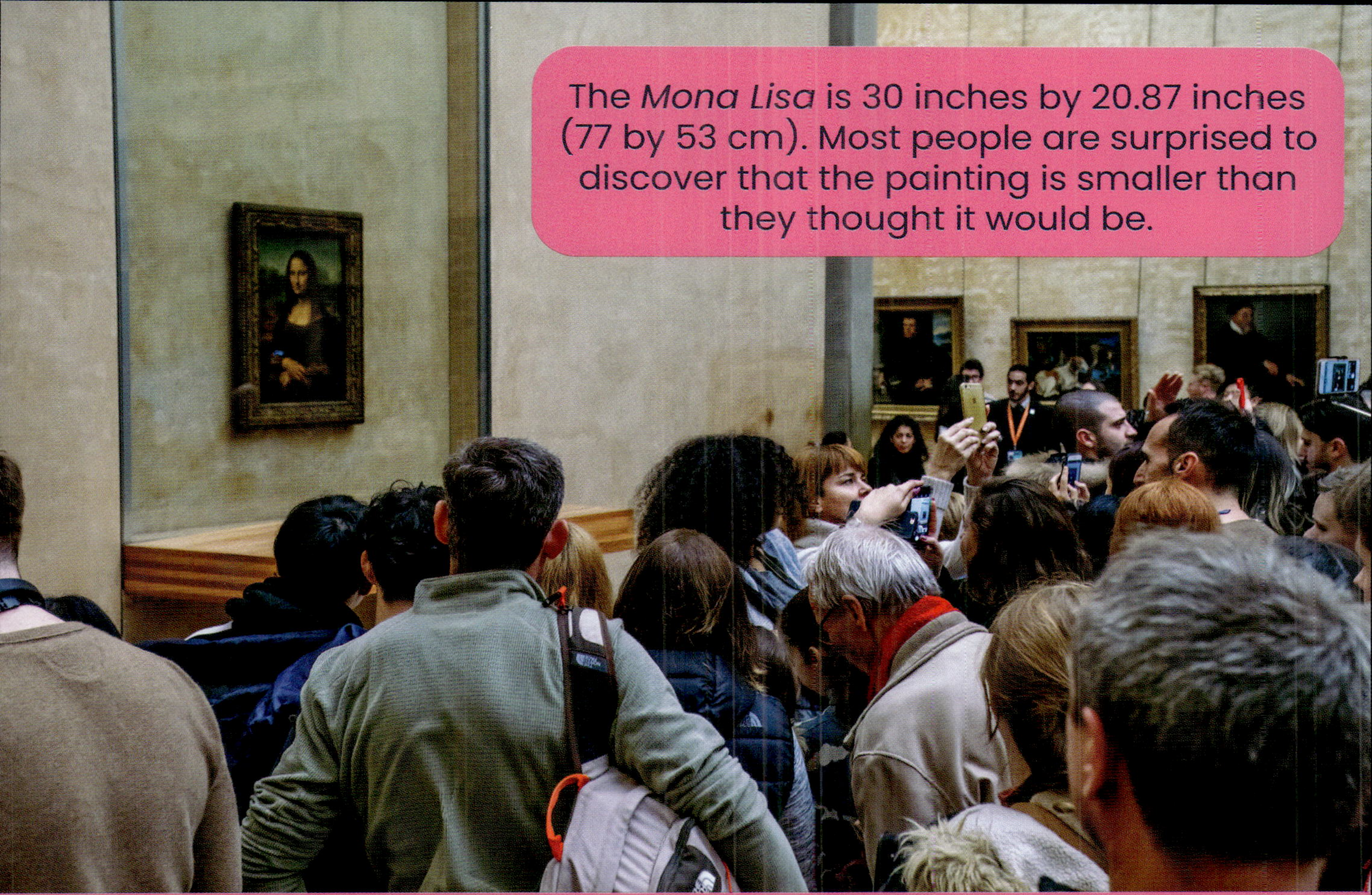

The *Mona Lisa* is 30 inches by 20.87 inches (77 by 53 cm). Most people are surprised to discover that the painting is smaller than they thought it would be.

Famous Quotes

Many notable people have written, spoken, and sung songs about the *Mona Lisa*. British art historian Kenneth Clark noted, "The *Mona Lisa* is the most famous, the most visited, the most written about, the most sung about, the most parodied work of art in the world." Nat King Cole famously crooned, "Are you warm, are you real, *Mona Lisa*, or just a cold and lonely, lovely work of art?"

THE RENAISSANCE

The Renaissance was a period in European history that started in Italy in the 1300s. This followed the Middle Ages, an era marked by a turning away from knowledge, art, and culture. Religion was far more important than individual people, art, and culture during the Middle Ages.

ARTI-FACT!

The Italian writers Francesco Petrarch and Giovanni Boccaccio are often credited with initiating the humanist movement. They began to explore these beliefs in writings from ancient Greece and Rome. Their enthusiasm quickly spread to other writers and artists.

Renaissance artists were skilled in creating highly detailed human forms, and nudity became more common and acceptable in art.

The Renaissance was a time of renewed interest in ancient cultures, as well as a blossoming of art and science. It marked the rise of humanism, a philosophy that places **self-realization** and artistic expression above supernatural beliefs. Although Christianity remained important in Europe, artists began displaying figures from Christianity, as well as Greek and Roman mythology, as real people.

The artists, writers, and thinkers of the Renaissance became interested in what ancient people thought about humanity. This renewed interest in the past also affected the sciences. For example, around 1543, Polish astronomer Nicolaus Copernicus stunned the science world by claiming the sun, and not Earth, is at the center of the solar system. New ways of thinking and artistic freedom resulted in an era of high art and scientific advancement.

Da Vinci's art, as well as the art of many other Renaissance artists, is priceless today. The *Mona Lisa* is a treasured work of art, but it's also an artifact because it displays human craftsmanship.

The House of Medici

The Medicis of Florence, Italy, rose to power as wool merchants and bankers. They funded many projects—paintings, sculptures, books, buildings, and more. They funded the building of the Uffizi Gallery in Florence, where the Medici family's personal art collection is displayed today. Although many historians believe the Medicis were **corrupt**, one can't deny the great contributions they made to art and science during the Renaissance.

This Renaissance painting by Raphael shows three members of the Medici family: Pope Leo X (center), Cardinal Giulio de' Medici (left), and Cardinal Luigi de' Rossi (right).

THE ITALIAN POLYMATH

Leonardo da Vinci was born April 15, 1452, near the town of Vinci. Around age 14, he became an assistant to the artist Verrocchio. He learned many important painting skills, but he also learned about **metallurgy**, leather working, carpentry, chemistry, and more.

There wasn't much da Vinci couldn't do! Even after he had become a famous artist, he continued to gain knowledge. He became a musician. He mastered mathematics in his thirties. He was a drafter, sculptor, architect, engineer, and more! His famous paintings include *The Last Supper*, *The Vitruvian Man*, and of course the *Mona Lisa*.

ARTI-FACT!

A "Renaissance man" is someone with a large range of interests and skills, and is an expert on numerous topics. Another word for this is "polymath." Da Vinci was perhaps the greatest Renaissance man who ever lived!

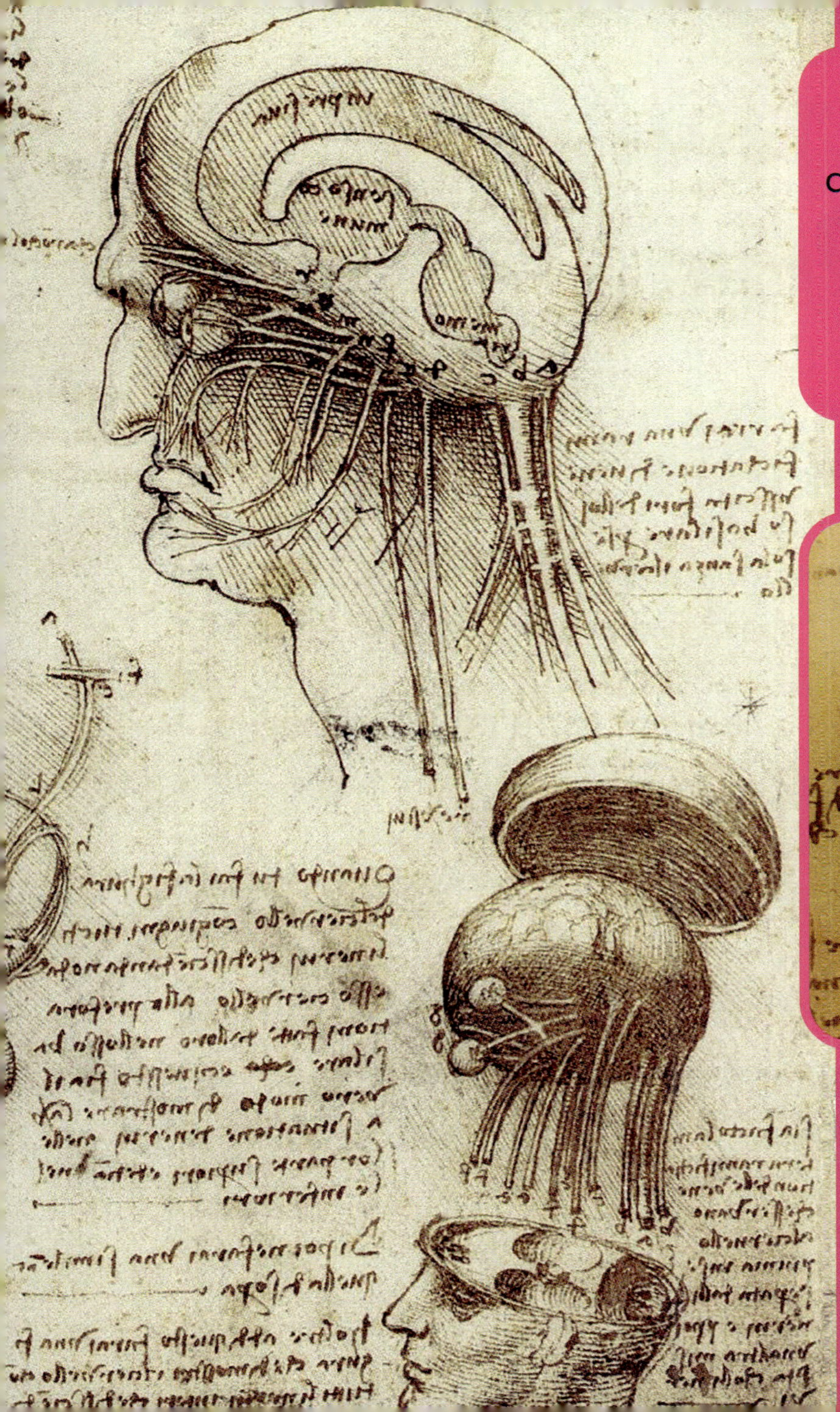

In addition to painting, da Vinci created many detailed sketches of human **anatomy**, animals, plants, landscapes, mechanical devices, and even a flying machine similar to a modern helicopter.

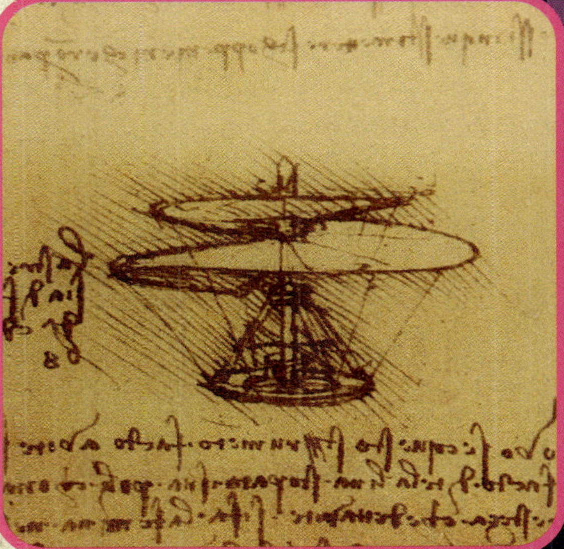

PAINTING THE *MONA LISA*

There are a few theories about who the person was that posed for da Vinci's painting. However, most historians believe it was Lisa del Giocondo, wife of Florentine silk merchant Francesco del Giocondo. Del Giocondo **commissioned** da Vinci to create a painting of his wife, who had recently given birth to their fifth child, something they wanted to celebrate.

Da Vinci started the painting in 1503. He used oil paints on a panel of white poplar. Many sources say he completed the painting in 1506, but studies of the painting show that da Vinci may have added to it up until his death in 1519.

Italian artist Cesare Maccari (1840–1919) painted *Leonardo Painting the Mona Lisa* in 1863.

Mona Lisa's pose was **unorthodox** for the 1500s. She is turned toward and looking at the viewer, increasing our interest in her. Other artists of the time copied this pose in their own paintings.

Da Vinci applied many layers of tiny brush strokes to create a soft blending of colors. This can be seen at the corners of *Mona Lisa's* eyes and mouth, and in the background. This is a technique da Vinci created known as sfumato (from the Italian word *sfumare*, or "to evaporate like smoke"). This creates a life-like feeling of depth and warmth. Other artists would begin to copy this technique as well.

Da Vinci's work displays a deep understanding of human anatomy. A close look at *Mona Lisa's* left eye, for example, shows a small bump that doctors call a xanthelasma, which is a **cholesterol** deposit and possible sign of heart disease.

DA VINCI'S LATER YEARS

For the last 14 years of his life, da Vinci traveled to work in places other than Florence, including Milan and Rome. In 1516, French king François I invited da Vinci to France. He moved to Amboise, France, and stayed there until he died in 1519. This whole time, da Vinci carried the *Mona Lisa* with him wherever he went.

After da Vinci died, François I bought the painting. It was part of the royal art collection but was moved to the Louvre after the end of the French Revolution (1789–1799). From 1800 to 1804, French Emperor Napoleon Bonaparte ordered that the *Mona Lisa* be moved to his personal bedroom.

ARTI-FACT!

The *Mona Lisa* remained in da Vinci's possession until his death. That means he never delivered it to del Giocondo, the man who paid for it!

Students of da Vinci made **replicas** of the *Mona Lisa* during his lifetime. The famous Renaissance painter Raphael even made a sketch of the painting, which has been displayed in the Louvre near the *Mona Lisa*.

RISING FAME

The *Mona Lisa* was placed in the Grand Gallery of the Louvre in 1804. The initial interest in the painting faded quickly. However, the portrait was "rediscovered" by French and English writers in the mid-1800s.

Theories arose regarding the woman's smile. Did she have bad teeth and didn't want to show them? They also asked: Why is she seated the way she is? Why does she seem to be gazing back at the viewer? Why doesn't she have eyebrows? These questions added to the mystery and mystique behind the painting, as viewers tried to understand what *Mona Lisa* was thinking.

No Eyebrows?

The painter Salvador Dalí once commented: "Mona Lisa has no eyebrows. I wonder what happened to them." Many others have wondered this as well. Perhaps it was a popular beauty trend of the 16th century in Italy. Maybe the paint faded over the years. Or maybe the eyebrows were accidentally removed by a poor **restoration** effort. Whatever the reason, the lack of eyebrows has only added to the mystery of the painting.

This is a 1911 painting by French artist Louis Béroud (1852–1930). He had been sketching the *Mona Lisa* in the Louvre and came in one morning to find the portrait missing!

KIDNAPPED!

Despite it's newfound fame, the *Mona Lisa* was not yet a star. However, something happened in 1911 that would cause her fame to skyrocket.

Vincenzo Peruggia was an Italian man working at the Louvre. He stole the painting because he felt it belonged in Italy. He hid it for two years before showing it to an Italian art dealer. It was displayed in the Uffizi Gallery in Florence for two weeks. Soon after, the *Mona Lisa* was returned to the Louvre. Peruggia spent 6 months in jail. The theft put *Mona Lisa* on the front page of newspapers all over the world.

ARTI-FACT!

Mona Lisa is short for "Madonna Lisa," or "my lady Lisa." In France, the painting is called *La Joconde*, which means "amused woman." It's also a reference to the woman's last name—Giocondo.

Mona Lisa became a celebrity after the theft! People suddenly wanted to know what was so great about the painting.

A PLACE OF HER OWN

After *Mona Lisa* rose to fame, she traveled to other countries, including the United States, the Soviet Union (Russia today), and Japan.

The Louvre has about 9 million visitors a year. The *Mona Lisa* is the biggest attraction with an average of 20,000 visitors a day! In 2026, Louvre officials announced a new **expansion** to help reduce crowd problems. The *Mona Lisa* will receive her own 33,000-square-foot (3,066 sq m) exhibition space that people can visit without visiting the rest of the museum. Officials hope this will make it easier to get to and see the *Mona Lisa*, while making the rest of the museum less crowded.

LOUVRE MUSEUM OF ARTS

The *Mona Lisa* is surrounded by crowds of museum-goers all day long, every day.

Mona Lisa Under Glass

Today, the *Mona Lisa* is behind protective glass—for a good reason. In 1956, someone tried to slice the painting with a razor, and another person hit it with a rock. In 1974 while in Tokyo, someone sprayed red paint at the portrait. In 2009, someone threw a teacup at the painting. In 2022, someone smeared cake on the *Mona Lisa*. In 2024, after glass was put over the painting, climate **activists** threw soup at the painting.

OFTEN COPIED...

The *Mona Lisa's* likeness has been copied and parodied many times over the years. Her likeness is in the public domain, meaning the no one owns it and no permission is needed to use it. It didn't take long for artists to use her likeness to create new works of art.

How do you feel about artists reusing the *Mona Lisa's* likeness in their paintings. Is it still art? Is it lazy, smart, creative, or something else?

ANDY WARHOL

French artist Marcel Duchamp (1887–1968) was perhaps the first artist to use the *Mona Lisa* in his own creation. This *Mona Lisa* has a mustache!

MONA LISA AS PRINCESS LEIA

GRAFFITI ART

In addition to copies and parodies, the *Mona Lisa* has been used to sell products. This is an effective advertising **strategy** because the *Mona Lisa* is so well known all over the world. And of course, her likeness is in the public domain so companies don't need to pay for it.

What do you think about using famous paintings to advertise products? Some people think it's bad to cheapen famous images like that. Some people think using art as advertisement is a good thing. It shows that the art can still grab a person's attention. What do you think?

ARTI-FACT!

The *Mona Lisa* has been honored in another way—by naming things after her! This includes several species of flowers and several ships.

The rock group The Beatles used the *Mona Lisa* on a concert poster in 1968.

...NEVER DUPLICATED

Louis Armstrong once told an interviewer, "A lotta cats copy the *Mona Lisa*, but people still line up to see the original." He was referring to musicians who copied his musical style, but he used the *Mona Lisa* as a common comparison that everyone was familiar with.

While there have been many copies of the *Mona Lisa* over the years, there's still just one *Mona Lisa*. And of all the copies, very few are considered an artifact the way the *Mona Lisa* is. This mysterious painting will continue to intrigue, entertain, and sell products for years to come!

TIMELINE

1200s	The Medici family of Florence rises to power.
1300s	The Renaissance begins in Italy.
April 15, 1452	Leonardo da Vinci is born.
1503	Da Vinci begins painting the *Mona Lisa*.
1506	Some sources say da Vinci finishes the painting.
1516	Da Vinci moves to France.
May 2, 1519	Da Vinci dies.
1804	The *Mona Lisa* moves to the Louvre.
1911	The *Mona Lisa* is stolen.
2026	The Louvre announces plans to give the *Mona Lisa* a place of her own in the museum.

GLOSSARY

activist: A person who believes in forceful action for political purposes.
anatomy: The structural makeup of an organism.
cholesterol: A waxy substance present in animal cells and tissues that is important in bodily processes. Too much cholesterol in one's diet can cause health problems.
commission: Order to be made.
corrupt: Characterized by immoral or illegal conduct.
expansion: The act or process of making a building bigger.
metallurgy: The science of metals.
mystique: A sense of mystery and respect around something or someone.
parody: A work of writing, art, or music in which the style of the original artist or work is imitated, often for comic effect.
replica: An exact or very close copy of something.
restoration: Having to do with returning something to it's original state, or as close as possible.
self-realization: The act of achieving the full development of your abilities and talents.
strategy: A careful plan or method.
unorthodox: Different from what is usually done or accepted.

FOR MORE INFORMATION

BOOKS

Day, Nicholas. *The Mona Lisa Vanishes: A Legendary Painter, a Shocking Heist, and the Birth of a Global Celebrity*. New York, NY: Random House Studio, 2025.

O'Neal, Ciara. *The Story of Leonardo da Vinci: An Inspiring Biography for Young Readers*. New York, NY: Calisto Kids, 2021.

WEBSITES

Louvre
www.louvre.fr/en
Explore the Louvre Museum online!

Renaissance for Kids
www.ducksters.com/history/renaissance.php
The Ducksters website has a wealth of information about the Renaissance, including government, daily life, culture, and famous people.

INDEX